Hat Crochet Tutorials

Crochet Your Own Hat With Amazing Pattern

Copyright © 2021

All rights reserved.

DEDICATION

Contents

Simple Seed Stitch Beanie Crochet Hat Pattern For Men, Women, and Kids for Christmas

Keep the men and boys in your home cozy this winter with a quick and easy to make seed stitch beanie! The seed stitch adds texture and warmth to the beanie, helping to protect heads of all sizes from winter winds.

Because the seed stitch beanie is a quick and easy crochet project to work up it would be perfect for last minute Christmas gifts, or donating to charities that help the homeless and needy this winter.

TERMINOLOGY AND PREP

Difficulty:

Easy

Materials Needed:

5.5mm hook, or hook needed to obtain gauge

150-225 yards Caron One Pound, or other thicker #4 worsted weight yarn in the colors of your choice

Yarn needle

Scissors

6"X6" piece of faux fur for pom-pom – optional

Stitches Used:

ch = chain

sl st = slip stitch

sc = single crochet

hdc = half double crochet

dc = double crochet

FPsc = front post single crochet

BPsc = back post single crochet

Additional Terms:

Working in the 3rd Loop of hdc – Instructions: Look at the top of the stitch, and locate the sideways "V", bend the stitch to look at the back*, and you should see another "V". You'll be working into the back loop of that "V", this is called the 3rd loop.

Gauge:

13 hdc sts in 4"; hdc stitches should be 1/2" tall. Circle should measure 3 1/2" across after round 4, 4 1/4" after round 5, and 5" across after round 6.

Measurements:

Large/X-Large Adult hat: 8 1/2" tall by 10 1/2" wide

Medium Adult hat: 8" tall by 10" wide

Teen/Small Adult: 8" tall by 9 ½" wide

6-10 yrs Child's hat 7 3/4" tall by 9" wide

ADDITIONAL NOTES:

-First st of round should be made in the same st as join.

-You will need to use a thicker worsted weight yarn to achieve the size measurements listed. Making a gauge swatch before you start should help.

-This hat is primarily crocheted using the Seed Stitch. Every round you make, except for the ribbing, will alternate dc, and sc sts. The non-increase rounds will stack dc on top of sc and vice versa, but the increase rounds will not. Keep alternating anyway.

-Size can be adjusted down slightly by using a 5mm (H) hook if these sizes are not quite the right fit.

-Optional Finishing details: Earflaps/Ties, or faux fur pom-pom are listed at the end of the pattern.

HOW TO MAKE A LARGE/X-LARGE SEED STITCH BEANIE

Pattern Instructions (US Terms):

Large/X-Large Adult size (fits 24"-25" heads):

ROUNDS 1-6

Round 1: ch 1, [dc, sc] 4 times in magic circle, join with sl st to first dc.

(8)

Round 2: ch 1, (sc, dc) in each st around, join with sl st to first sc. (16)

Round 3: ch 1, (dc, sc), in first st, dc in next st, (sc, dc) in next st, sc in next st * dc, sc), in next st, dc in next st, (sc, dc) in next st, sc in next st; repeat from * around, join with sl st to first dc. (24)

Round 4: ch 1, (sc, dc) in first st, sc in next st, dc in next st *(sc, dc) in next st, sc in next st, dc in next st; repeat from * around, join with sl st to first sc. (32)

Round 5: ch 1, (dc, sc) in first st, dc in next st, sc in next st, dc in next st, (sc, dc) in next st, sc in next st, dc in next st, sc in next st *(dc, sc) in next st, dc in next st, sc in next st, dc in next st, (sc, dc) in next st, sc in next st, dc in next st, sc in next st; repeat from * around, join with sl st to first dc. (40)

Round 6: ch 1: (sc, dc) in first st, [sc in next st, dc in next st] 2 times *(sc, dc) in next st, [sc in next st, dc in next st] 2 times; repeat from * around, join with sl st to first sc. (48)

ROUNDS 7-12

Round 7: ch 1, (dc, sc) in first st, dc in next st, sc in next st, dc in next st, sc in next st, dc in next st, (sc, dc) in next st, sc in next st, dc in next st, sc in next st, dc in next st, sc in next st *(dc, sc) in next st, dc in next st, sc in next st, dc in next st, sc in next st, dc in next st, (sc, dc) in next st, sc in next st, dc in next st, sc in next st, dc in next st, sc in next st; repeat from * around, join with sl st to first dc. (56)

Round 8: ch 1, (sc, dc) in first st, [sc in next st, dc in next st] 3 times *(sc, dc) in next st, [sc in next st, dc in next st] 3 times; repeat from * around, join with sl st to first sc. (64)

Round 9: ch 1, (dc, sc) in first st, [dc in next st, sc in next st] 3 times, dc in next st, (sc, dc) in next st [sc in next st, dc in next st] 3 times, sc in next st *(dc, sc) in first st, [dc in next st, sc in next st] 3 times, dc in next st, (sc, dc) in next st [sc in next st, dc in next st] 3 times, sc in next st; repeat from * around, join with sl st to first dc. (72)

7

Round 10: ch 1, hdc in each st around, join with sl st to first hdc. (72)

Round 11: ch 1, working in 3rd loop of hdc, hdc in each st around, join with sl st to first hdc. (72)

Round 12: ch 1, working in 3rd loop of hdc, sc in each st around, join with sl st to first sc. (64, 72)

ROUNDS 13-21

Round 13: ch 1, sc in first st, dc in next st *sc in next st, dc in next st; repeat from * around, join with sl st to first sc. (72)

Round 14: ch 1, dc in first st, sc in next st *dc in next st, sc in next st; repeat from * around, join with sl st to first dc. (72)

Round 15: ch 1, sc in first st, dc in next st *sc in next st, dc in next st; repeat from * around, join with sl st to first sc. (72)

Rounds 16-21: Repeat rounds 10-15 one more time

ROUND 22-27

Rounds 22-24: Repeat rounds 10-12 one more time

Round 25: ch 1, FPsc around first st, BPsc around next st *FPsc around next st, BPsc around next st; repeat from * around, join with sl st to first FPsc. (72)

Rounds 26-27: ch 1, *FPsc around FPsc from prev round, sc in next st; repeat from * around, join with sl st to first FPsc. (72)

Your hat should measure at least 8 1/2" long by this point. If not, feel free to repeat round 26 again.

Fasten off and weave in ends.

HOW TO MAKE A MEDIUM SIZE SEED STITCH BEANIE

Medium Adult size (22"-23" heads):

ROUNDS 1-6

Round 1: ch 1, [dc, sc] 4 times in magic circle, join with sl st to first dc. (8)

Round 2: ch 1, (sc, dc) in each st around, join with sl st to first sc. (16)

Round 3: ch 1, (dc, sc), in first st, dc in next st, (sc, dc) in next st, sc in next st * dc, sc), in next st, dc in next st, (sc, dc) in next st, sc in next st; repeat from * around, join with sl st to first dc. (24)

Round 4: ch 1, (sc, dc) in first st, sc in next st, dc in next st *(sc, dc) in next st, sc in next st, dc in next st; repeat from * around, join with sl st to first sc. (32)

Round 5: ch 1, (dc, sc) in first st, dc in next st, sc in next st, dc in next st, (sc, dc) in next st, sc in next st, dc in next st, sc in next st *(dc, sc) in next st, dc in next st, sc in next st, dc in next st, (sc, dc) in next st, sc in next st, dc in next st, sc in next st; repeat from * around, join with sl st to first dc. (40)

Round 6: ch 1: (sc, dc) in first st, [sc in next st, dc in next st] 2 times *(sc, dc) in next st, [sc in next st, dc in next st] 2 times; repeat from * around, join with sl st to first sc. (48)

ROUNDS 7-10

Round 7: ch 1, (dc, sc) in first st, dc in next st, sc in next st, dc in next st, sc in next st, dc in next st, (sc, dc) in next st, sc in next st, dc in next st, sc in next st, dc in next st, sc in next st *(dc, sc) in next st, dc in next st, sc in next st, dc in next st, sc in next st, dc in next st, (sc, dc) in next st, sc in next st, dc in next st, sc in next st, dc in next st, sc in next st; repeat from * around, join with sl st to first dc. (56)

Round 8: ch 1, (sc, dc) in first st, [sc in next st, dc in next st] 3 times *(sc, dc) in next st, [sc in next st, dc in next st] 3 times; repeat from * around, join with sl st to first sc. (64)

Round 9: ch 1, hdc in each st around, join with sl st to first hdc. (64)

Round 10: ch 1, working in 3rd loop of hdc, hdc in each st around, join with sl st to first hdc. (64)

ROUNDS 11-14

Round 11: ch 1, working in 3rd loop of hdc, sc in each st around, join with sl st to first sc. (64)

Round 12: ch 1, sc in first st, dc in next st *sc in next st, dc in next st; repeat from * around, join

with sl st to first sc. (64)

Round 13: ch 1, dc in first st, sc in next st *dc in next st, sc in next st; repeat from * around, join with sl st to first dc. (64)

Round 14: ch 1, sc in first st, dc in next st *sc in next st, dc in next st; repeat from * around, join with sl st to first sc. (64)

ROUND 15-25

Rounds 15-20: Repeat rounds 9-14 one more time

Rounds 21-23: Repeat rounds 9-11 one more time

Round 24: ch 1, FPsc around first st, BPsc around next st *FPsc around next st, BPsc around next st; repeat from * around, join with sl st to first FPsc. (64)

Round 25: ch 1, *FPsc around FPsc from prev round, sc in next st; repeat from * around, join with sl st to first FPsc. (64)

Fasten off, and weave in ends.

HOW TO MAKE A TEEN/SMALL ADULT SEED STITCH

BEANIE

Teen/Small Adult size (21-22" heads):

ROUNDS 1-6

Round 1: ch 1, [dc, sc] 4 times in magic circle, join with sl st to first dc. (8)

Round 2: ch 1, (sc, dc) in each st around, join with sl st to first sc. (16)

Round 3: ch 1, (dc, sc), in first st, dc in next st, (sc, dc) in next st, sc in next st * dc, sc), in next st, dc in next st, (sc, dc) in next st, sc in next st; repeat from * around, join with sl st to first dc. (24)

Round 4: ch 1, (sc, dc) in first st, sc in next st, dc in next st *(sc, dc) in next st, sc in next st, dc in next st; repeat from * around, join with sl st to first sc. (32)

Round 5: ch 1, (dc, sc) in first st, dc in next st, sc in next st, dc in next st, (sc, dc) in next st, sc in next st, dc in next st, sc in next st *(dc, sc) in next st, dc in next st, sc in next st, dc in next st, (sc, dc) in next st, sc in next st, dc in next st, sc in next st; repeat from * around, join with sl st to first dc. (40)

Round 6: ch 1: (sc, dc) in first st, [sc in next st, dc in next st] 2 times *(sc, dc) in next st, [sc in next st, dc in next st] 2 times; repeat from * around, join with sl st to first sc. (48)

ROUNDS 7-10

Round 7: ch 1, (dc, sc) in first st, dc in next st, sc in next st, dc in next st, sc in next st, dc in next st, (sc, dc) in next st, sc in next st, dc in next st, sc in next st, dc in next st, sc in next st *(dc, sc) in next st, dc in next st, sc in next st, dc in next st, sc in next st, dc in next st, (sc, dc) in next st, sc in next st, dc in next st, sc in next st, dc in next st, sc in next st; repeat from * around, join with sl st to first dc. (56)

Round 8: ch 1, (sc, dc) in first st, [sc in next st, dc in next st] 5 times, *(sc, dc) in next st, [sc in next st, dc in next st] 5 times; repeat from * around, join with sl st to first sc. (60)

15

Round 9: ch 1, hdc in each st around, join with sl st to first hdc. (60)

Round 10: ch 1, working in 3rd loop of hdc, hdc in each st around, join with sl st to first hdc. (60)

ROUNDS 11-14

Round 11: ch 1, working in 3rd loop of hdc, sc in each st around, join with sl st to first sc. (60)

Round 12: ch 1, sc in first st, dc in next st *sc in next st, dc in next st; repeat from * around, join with sl st to first sc. (60)

Round 13: ch 1, dc in first st, sc in next st *dc in next st, sc in next st; repeat from * around, join with sl st to first dc. (60)

Round 14: ch 1, sc in first st, dc in next st *sc in next st, dc in next st; repeat from * around, join with sl st to first sc. (60)

ROUND 15-25

Rounds 15-20: Repeat rounds 9-14 one more time

Rounds 21-23: Repeat rounds 9-11 one more time

Round 24: ch 1, FPsc around first st, BPsc around next st *FPsc around next st, BPsc around next st; repeat from * around, join with sl st to first FPsc. (60)

Round 25: ch 1, *FPsc around FPsc from prev round, sc in next st; repeat from * around, join with sl st to first FPsc. (60)

Fasten off, and then weave in ends.

HOW TO MAKE A CHILD SIZE SEED STITCH BEANIE

Child's size (6-10 yrs, 18"-21" heads):

ROUNDS 1-6

Round 1: ch 1, [dc, sc] 4 times in magic circle, join with sl st to first dc. (8)

Round 2: ch 1, (sc, dc) in each st around, join with sl st to first sc. (16)

Round 3: ch 1, (dc, sc), in first st, dc in next st, (sc, dc) in next st, sc in next st * dc, sc), in next st, dc in next st, (sc, dc) in next st, sc in next st; repeat from * around, join with sl st to first dc. (24)

Round 4: ch 1, (sc, dc) in first st, sc in next st, dc in next st *(sc, dc) in next st, sc in next st, dc in next st; repeat from * around, join with sl st to first sc. (32)

Round 5: ch 1, (dc, sc) in first st, dc in next st, sc in next st, dc in next st, (sc, dc) in next st, sc in next st, dc in next st, sc in next st *(dc, sc) in next st, dc in next st, sc in next st, dc in next st, (sc, dc) in next st, sc in next st, dc in next st, sc in next st; repeat from * around, join with sl st to first dc. (40)

Round 6: ch 1: (sc, dc) in first st, [sc in next st, dc in next st] 2 times *(sc, dc) in next st, [sc in next st, dc in next st] 2 times; repeat from * around, join with sl st to first sc. (48)

ROUNDS 7-10

Round 7: ch 1, (dc, sc) in first st, dc in next st, sc in next st, dc in next st, sc in next st, dc in next st, (sc, dc) in next st, sc in next st, dc in next st, sc in next st, dc in next st, sc in next st *(dc, sc) in next st, dc in next st, sc in next st, dc in next st, sc in next st, dc in next st, (sc, dc) in next st, sc in next st, dc in next st, sc in next st, dc in next st, sc in next st; repeat from * around, join with sl st to first dc. (56)

Round 8: ch 1, hdc in each st around, join with sl st to first hdc. (56)

Round 9: ch 1, working in 3rd loop of hdc, hdc in each st around, join with sl st to first hdc. (56)

Round 10: ch 1, working in 3rd loop of hdc, sc in each st around, join with sl st to first sc. (56)

ROUNDS 11-13

Round 11: ch 1, sc in first st, dc in next st *sc in next st, dc in next st; repeat from * around, join with sl st to first sc. (56)

Round 12: ch 1, dc in first st, sc in next st *dc in next st, sc in next st; repeat from * around, join with sl st to first dc. (56)

Round 13: ch 1, sc in first st, dc in next st *sc in next st, dc in next st; repeat from * around, join with sl st to first sc. (56)

ROUND 14-24

Rounds 14-19: Repeat rounds 8-13 one more time

Rounds 20-22: Repeat rounds 8-10 one more time

Round 23: ch 1, FPsc around first st, BPsc around next st *FPsc around next st, BPsc around next st; repeat from * around, join with sl st to first FPsc. (56)

Round 24: ch 1, *FPsc around FPsc from prev round, sc in next st; repeat from * around, join with sl st to first FPsc. (56)

Fasten off, and weave in ends.

SEED STITCH BEANIE FINISHING SUGGESTIONS

Optional Finishing Instructions:

Earflaps (you'll need to make two) – Position them on opposite sides of the hat starting on final round of sc sts right after finishing final rib.

Adult:

after finishing round 23 (L/XL) or 22 (S/M),

ROWS

1: ch 1, sc in next 12 stitches, ch 1, turn (12)

2-4: sc in each stitch across, ch 1, turn (12)

5: sc2tog, sc in next 8 stitches, sc2tog, ch 1, turn (10)

6: sc in each stitch across, ch 1, turn (10)

7: sc2tog, sc in next 6 stitches, sc2tog, ch1, turn (8)

8: sc in each stitch across, turn (8)

9: sc2tog, sc in next 4 stitches, sc2tog, ch 1, turn (6)

10: sc in each stitch across, ch 1, turn (6)

11: sc2tog, dc in next 2 stitches, sc2tog (4)

Fasten off, and weave in ends.

Child:

after finishing round 21,

ROWS

1: ch 1, sc in next 11 stitches

2-4: ch 1 turn, sc in each stitch across (11)

5: ch 1, turn, sc2tog, sc in next 7 stitches, sc2tog (9)

6: ch 1, turn, sc in each stitch across (9)

7: ch 1, turn, sc2tog, sc in next 5 stitches, sc2tog (7)

8: ch 1, turn, sc in each stitch across (7)

7: ch 1, turn, sc2tog, dc in next 3 stitches, sc2tog (5)

TIES/BRAIDS

Attach yarn to bottom of earflap, stitch a chain as long as you want the ties to be, and sc in 2nd chain from hook, and in each stitch across. Attach securely to bottom of earflap I square knot the ends, then weave them back and forth a couple of times to weave in the ends so they don't

come out.

Or,

Cut 9, 2 ft lengths of yarn for each tie, thread them through the bottom of the earflaps, and braid. Fasten off with a piece of yarn wound around the bottom section of the braid.

Norah Hat Pattern. Holiday Stashdown CAL

NORAH HAT PATTERN

Supplies

Yarn: Yarnspirations. Bernat Pop! Bulky Yarn. 9.8 oz (280 g) and 147 yds (134 m). 100% Acrylic. Super Bulky Weight Yarn [6]. Machine wash in cool water, delicate setting. Tumble dry, low heat, delicate cycle.

Colors: 1 skein in Rich Rainbow 93026

Hook: 10 mm (M/N).

Finished Project Yardage: Adult Medium: 4.45 oz (127 g) / 67 yards (61 m).

Scissors, Yarn Needle, Stitch Marker

Difficulty Level

Easy

Finished Size

Hat height to brow approximately 9 inches X 21 inches circumference (adult medium)

Please see measurements for the other sizes (Adult Large, Adult Small and Child) listed in the pattern below.

Gauge

Approximately 1.5 rows per inch and 1.5 stitches per inch

You can substitute any yarn and hook for this stitch pattern – just remember when you substitute if your gauge is different, the finished size, and amount of yarn used for your project will also be different.

Abbreviations

US Terminology used

beg – beginning

BL – back loop

ch – chain

dc – double crochet

DMR – double magic ring

hdc – half double crochet

R – round

rem – remaining

rep – repeat

sc – single crochet

sk – skip

sl st – slip stitch

st/sts – stitch/stitches

* to **– Repeat the instructions between the asterisks the number of times indicated. This repeat will contain of multiple instructions.

[] – at the end of the row – the total number of stitches

() – important notes AND sets of stitches to be worked within one stitch, or space

Notes:

Worked in continuous rounds. You may wish to use a stitch marker to mark your place.

If you crochet tightly you may wish to go up 1 hook size. Please check your gauge to be sure you are getting 3 stitches in every 2 inches and 3 rows in every 2 inches.

This hat is crocheted in one piece, in continuous rounds, from the crown down to the forehead.

Child (6-10 years)

Inner Hat Circumference: 19 inches (stretches + 2 inches)

Hat Height: 8 inches from crown to brow, 9 inches from crown to base of earflap

Using your 10 mm (N/P) hook (or size required for gauge) :

R1: DMR: 6 sc. [6 sc]

R2: 1 sc and 1 dc in each st around. [6 sc and 6 dc]

R3: *(1 sc and 1 dc) in the first st, 1 sc in the next st**. Rep from * to ** around. [12 sc and 6 dc]

R4: *(1 sc and 1 dc) in the first st, 1 sc in the next st, 1 dc in the next st**. Rep from * to ** around. [12 sc and 12 dc]

R5: *(1 sc and 1 dc) in the first st, 1 sc in the next st, 1 dc in the next st, 1 sc in the next st**. Rep from * to ** around. [18 sc and 12 dc]

R6: 1 sc in the first st. *1 sc in the next st, 1 dc in the next st**. Rep from * to ** around to the last st. 1 sc in the last st. [16 sc and 14 dc]

R7: 1 sc in the first st. *1 dc in the next st, 1 sc in the next st**. Rep from * to ** around to the last st. 1 dc in the last st. [15 sc and 15 dc]

R8-R9: Rep R6 and R7

R10: *1 sc in the BL of each of the next 5 sts, 1 sl st in the BL of each of the next 10 sts**. Rep from * to ** 2 times. [20 sl st and 10 sc]

R11: *1 hdc in the BL of the next st, 1 dc in the BL of each of the next 3 sts, 1 hdc in the BL of the next st, 1 sl st in the BL of each of the next 10 sts**. Rep from * to ** 2 times. [20 sl st, 4 hdc and 6 dc]

R12: *1 sc in the BL of each of the next 5 sts, 1 sl st in the BL of each of the next 10 sts**. Rep from * to ** 2 times. Finish off with an invisible join and weave in ends. [20 sl st, 10 sc]

Adult Small

Inner Hat Circumference: 20 inches (stretches + 2 inches)

Hat Height: 9 inches from crown to brow, 10 inches from crown to base of earflap

Using your 10 mm (N/P) hook (or size required for gauge) :

R1: DMR: 6 sc. [6 sc]

R2: 1 sc and 1 dc in each st around. [6 sc and 6 dc]

R3: *(1 sc and 1 dc) in the first st, 1 sc in the next st**. Rep from * to ** around. [12 sc and 6 dc]

R4: *(1 sc and 1 dc) in the first st, 1 sc in the next st, 1 dc in the next st**. Rep from * to ** around. [12 sc and 12 dc]

R5: *(1 sc and 1 dc) in the first st, 1 sc in the next st, 1 dc in the next st, 1 sc in the next st**. Rep from * to ** around. [18 sc and 12 dc]

R6: 1 sc in the first st. *1 sc in the next st, 1 dc in the next st**. Rep from * to ** around to the last st. 1 sc in the last st. [16 sc and 14 dc]

R7: 1 sc in the first st. *1 dc in the next st, 1 sc in the next st**. Rep from * to ** around to the last st. 1 dc in the last st. [15 sc and 15 dc]

R8-R11: Rep R6 and R7

R12: *1 sc in the BL of each of the next 5 sts, 1 sl st in the BL of each of the next 10 sts**. Rep from * to ** 2 times. [20 sl st and 10 sc]

R13: *1 hdc in the BL of the next st, 1 dc in the BL of each of the next 3 sts, 1 hdc in the BL of the next st, 1 sl st in the BL of each of the next 10 sts**. Rep from * to ** 2 times. [20 sl st, 4 hdc and 6 dc]

R14: *1 sc in the BL of each of the next 5 sts, 1 sl st in the BL of each of the next 10 sts**. Rep from * to ** 2 times. Finish off with an invisible join and weave in ends. [20 sl st, 10 sc]

Adult Medium

Inner Hat Circumference: 21 inches (stretches + 2 inches)

Hat Height: 9.5 inches from crown to brow, 10.5 inches from crown to base of earflap

Using your 10 mm (N/P) hook (or size required for gauge) :

R1: DMR: 6 sc. [6 sc]

R2: 1 sc and 1 dc in each st around. [6 sc and 6 dc]

R3: *(1 sc and 1 dc) in the first st, 1 sc in the next st**. Rep from * to ** around. [12 sc and 6 dc]

R4: *(1 sc and 1 dc) in the first st, 1 sc in the next st, 1 dc in the next st**. Rep from * to ** around. [12 sc and 12 dc]

R5: *(1 sc and 1 dc) in the first st, 1 sc in the next st, 1 dc in the next st, 1 sc in the next st**. Rep from * to ** around. [18 sc and 12 dc]

R6: *(1 sc and 1 dc) in the first st, 1 sc in the next st, 1 dc in the next st, 1 sc in the next st, 1 dc in the next st**. Rep from * to ** 2 times. (1 sc in the next st, 1 dc in the next st) around. [16 sc and 16 dc]

R7: 1 sc in the first st. *1 sc in the next st, 1 dc in the next st**. Rep from * to ** around to the last st. 1 sc in the last st. [17 sc and 15 dc]

R8: 1 sc in the first st. *1 dc in the next st, 1 sc in the next st**. Rep from * to ** around to the last st. 1 dc in the last st. [16 sc and 16 dc]

R9-R12: Rep R7 and R8

R13: *1 sc in the BL of each of the next 6 sts, 1 sl st in the BL of each of the next 10 sts**. Rep from * to ** 2 times. [20 sl st and 12 sc]

R14: *1 hdc in the BL of the next st, 1 dc in the BL of each of the next 4 sts, 1 hdc in the BL of the next st, 1 sl st in the BL of each of the next 10 sts**. Rep from * to ** 2 times. [20 sl st, 4 hdc and 8 dc] `

R15: *1 sc in the BL of each of the next 6 sts, 1 sl st in the BL of each of the next 10 sts**. Rep from * to ** 2 times. Finish off with an invisible join and weave in ends. [20 sl st, 12 sc]

Adult Large

Inner Hat Circumference: 22 inches (stretches + 2 inches)

Hat Height: 10 inches from crown to brow, 11 inches from crown to base of earflap

Using your 10 mm (N/P) hook (or size required for gauge) :

R1: DMR: 6 sc. [6 sc]

R2: 1 sc and 1 dc in each st around. [6 sc and 6 dc]

R3: *(1 sc and 1 dc) in the first st, 1 sc in the next st**. Rep from * to ** around. [12 sc and 6 dc]

R4: *(1 sc and 1 dc) in the first st, 1 sc in the next st, 1 dc in the next st**. Rep from * to ** around. [12 sc and 12 dc]

R5: *(1 sc and 1 dc) in the first st, 1 sc in the next st, 1 dc in the next st, 1 sc in the next st**. Rep from * to ** around. [18 sc and 12 dc]

R6: *(1 sc and 1 dc) in the first st, 1 sc in the next st, 1 dc in the next st, 1 sc in the next st, 1 dc in the next st**. Rep from * to ** 4 times. (1 sc in the next st, 1 dc in the next st) around. [17 sc and 17 dc]

R7: 1 sc in the first st. *1 sc in the next st, 1 dc in the next st**. Rep from * to ** around to the last st. 1 sc in the last st. [18 sc and 16 dc]

R8: 1 sc in the first st. *1 dc in the next st, 1 sc in the next st**. Rep from * to ** around to the last st. 1 dc in the last st. [17 sc and 17 dc]

R9-R12: Rep R7 and R8

R13: Rep R7

R14: *1 sc in the BL of each of the next 6 sts, 1 sl st in the BL of each of the next 11 sts**. Rep from * to ** 2 times. [22 sl st and 12 sc]

R15: *1 hdc in the BL of the next st, 1 dc in the BL of each of the next 4 sts, 1 hdc in the BL of the next st, 1 sl st in the BL of each of the next 11 sts**. Rep from * to ** 2 times. [22 sl st, 4 hdc and 8 dc]

R16: *1 sc in the BL of each of the next 6 sts, 1 sl st in the BL of each of the next 11 sts**. Rep from * to ** 2 times. Finish off with an invisible join and weave in ends. [22 sl st, 12 sc]

Winter Horseback Riding Helmet Cover Pattern

Winter Horseback Riding Helmet Cover Pattern

Supplies

Yarn: Red Heart Super Saver Chunky. 5 oz (141 g) and 173 yds (158 m). 100% acrylic. Bulky Weight Yarn [5]. Machine wash warm; tumble dry; do not bleach; do not iron; dry cleanable.

Colors: 1 skein in Dark Orchid – E306_0776.

Hook: 8 mm (L-11). I used this hook.

Finished Project Yardage: One Size Fits Most less than 123 g (151 yds)

Scissors, Yarn Needle, Stitch Marker

Difficulty Level

Easy

Finished Size

26 inches circumference, 15 inches height

To Cover Horse Back Riding Helmets. Small to XL. For the large and XL size you may wish to repeat a few more rounds for length to allow it to reach to cover the base of the neck.

Gauge

Approximately 2 rounds per 1.5 inches and 2 sts per inch

You can substitute any yarn and hook for this stitch pattern – just remember when you substitute if your gauge is different, the finished size, and amount of yarn used for your project will also be different.

Abbreviations

US Terminology used

bef- before

beg – beginning

ch – chain

dc – double crochet

DMR – double magic ring

R – round

rem – remaining

rep – repeat

sc – single crochet

sk – skip

sl st – slip stitch

sp – space

st/sts – stitch/stitches

* to **– Repeat the instructions between the asterisks the number of times indicated. This repeat will contain of multiple instructions.

[] – at the end of the row – the total number of stitches

() – important notes AND sets of stitches to be worked within one stitch, or space

The helmet cover is worked in joined rounds from the crown (top) of the hat, downward.

Part 1. The Main Hat.

Using your 8 mm (L-11) hook (or size required for gauge).

R1: In a DMR, ch 3 and work 12 dc. Sl st to the first dc of the round to join. [12]

R2: Ch 3, 2 dc in each dc around. Sl st to the first dc to join. [24]

R3: Ch 3, *2 dc in the next st, 1 dc in the next st**. Rep from * to ** around. Sl st to the first dc of the round to join. [36]

R4: Ch 3, *2 dc in the next st, 1 dc in each of the next 2 sts**. Rep from * to ** around. Sl st to the first dc of the round to join. [48]

R5-R9: Ch 3, 1 dc in each st around. Sl st to the first dc of the round to join. [48]

R10: Ch 3, 1 dc in each of the next 16 sts, ch 14, sk 14 sts, 1 dc in each of the remaining 18 sts. Sl st to the first dc of the round to join. [34 dc, 14 ch]

R11: Ch 3, 1 dc in each of the next 16 sts, 1 dc in the back bar of each of the 14 chs, 1 dc in each of the next 18 sts. Sl st to the first dc of the round to join. [48]

R12-19: Ch 3, 1 dc in each st around. Sl st to the first dc of the round to join. [48]

If you would like a longer hat, keep repeating until you reach your preferred length.

Finish off.

Part 2. The Helmet Brim / Peak Cover.

Using your 8 mm (L-11) hook (or size required for gauge).

With the hat facing you like this, with the RS facing out (toward you):

R1: Join your yarn with a standing dc stitch (Or you can join with a sl st and ch 3. If you use this sl st method you will need to count the ch 3 as a 1 dc) in the first sk ch from R10. 1 dc in each ch across. Turn. [14]

R2: Ch 3 (counts as 1 dc), 1 dc in each st across. Sl st to the next dc of the main hat. Ch 1 and turn. [14]

R3: 1 sc in each st across. Sl st to the next dc of the main hat. Ch 1, turn. [14]

R4: 1 sl st in each st across. Sl st to the same dc of the main hat (same as previous row). Finish off.

Finishing Instructions.

Tulip Stitch Crochet Hat Pattern

For Holiday

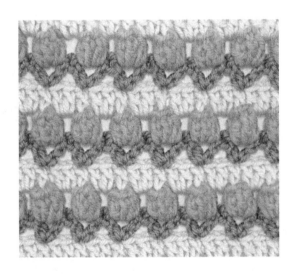

Supplies

Yarn: Chic Sheep by Marly Bird. Medium Weight Yarn [4]. 3.5 oz / 100 g. 186 yd / 170 m. 100% Mercerized Merino Wool. Machine wash cold, gentle cycle, lay flat to dry.

Colors: Color A: Linen, Color B: Polo and Color C: Mai Tai. The yellow used in the stitch tutorial is Mimosa.

Hook: 4 mm (G) and 5 mm (H) Crochet Hook (I used these hooks.)

Finished Project Yardage: Child: 75 g

Scissors, Yarn Needle, Stitch Marker

Difficulty Level

Easy-Intermediate

Finished Size

Please see all the size measurements listed in each section below. Preemie to Adult Large.

Gauge

approximately 16 dc per 4 inches (4 dc per inch)

approximately 9 rounds dc per 4 inches (2.25 rounds per inch)

You can substitute any yarn and hook for this stitch pattern – just remember when you substitute if your gauge is different, the finished size of your project will also be different.

Abbreviations

US Terminology used

beg – beginning

BL – back loop

ch – chain

ch1sp – chain 1 space

ch2sp – chain 2 space

dc – double crochet

dc2tog – double crochet 2 together

hdc – half double crochet

hdc2tog – half double crochet 2 together

pc – popcorn stitch

R – row

RS – Right Side ("good or pretty side you want to show")

rem – remaining

rep – repeat

sc – single crochet

sk – skip

sl st – slip stitch

st/sts – stitch/stitches

WS – wrong side (back of project)

* to **– Repeat the instructions between the asterisks the number of times indicated. This repeat will contain of multiple instructions.

[] – at the end of the row – the total number of stitches

() – important notes AND sets of stitches to be worked within one stitch, or space

Special Stitches

Popcorn Stitch (pc)

The popcorn stitch used in this pattern is made up of 5 dc stitches all crocheted into the same ch1sp. After you make the 5 dc stitches, remove the loop from the hook (see image below) and insert the hook through the top of the first dc stitch (under both the front and back loops of the stitch), from front to back (see image below). Reinsert your hook into the loop you removed (see image below). Draw that loop through the first dc stitch (already on your hook) to complete the popcorn stitch.

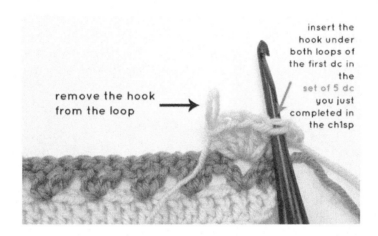

remove the hook from the loop

insert the hook under both loops of the first dc in the set of 5 dc you just completed in the ch1sp

Notes

Leave an 8-10 inch tail of yarn before you begin the band. You will use this tail of yarn to whipstitch the band closed after you finish the hat.

Ch 3 counts as 1 dc when worked at the beg of the row. This means you do not work into the st that falls beneath it.

If you do not wish to use a standing dc, please work a sl st join and ch 3 instead. This will count as 1 dc.

Finish off: ch 1, cut yarn and pull the yarn end through the loop

Sl st does not count as a stitch.

To increase the slouch of the hat add extra repeat sections (where we work 1 dc in each st around).

Stitch Multiple: 3

Color A: Linen, Color B: Polo and Color C: Mai Tai.

To fit 11-12 inch head circumference. Hat height approximately 4 inches.

The hat is crocheted from the ribbed band to the crown of the hat in one piece. We begin by crocheting the band, which is worked back and forth in rows.

With the smaller hook (4 mm [G]) and Color A

R1: Ch 3, 1 sc in each ch across, ch 1, turn. [2]

R2-R42: 1 sc in the BL (back loop) of the first st, 1 sc (under both loops) in the last st, ch 1, turn. [2]

Rotate your work to crochet across the top of the band (the row edges). We are working the main body of the hat next, using the larger hook.

The body of the hat is worked with the larger hook (5 mm [H]).

With Color A

R1: RS: Ch 3 (counts as 1 dc), 1 dc in each row end across (tip: work under one loop of yarn on the row ends). Sl st to the top of the ch 3 to join. Finish off leaving a tail of yarn for seaming. [42]

Turn your work (you will be working around the inside of the hat) and continue to R2 below using Yarn Color B.

R2: WS: Join yarn with 1 standing dc stitch (*see notes*), ch 1 and work 1 more dc in the same st. *Sk 2 dc, (1 dc, ch 1, 1 dc) in the next dc**. Rep from * to ** across to the last 2 dc. Sk the last 2 dc. Sl st to the top of the initial dc to join. Finish off Color B. [14 (1 dc, ch 1, 1 dc) sets]

Turn your work (you will be working around the outside of the hat) and continue to R3 below using Yarn Color C.

R3: RS: Join yarn with 1 standing dc in any ch1sp. Work 4 more dc in the same ch1sp. You will be making a pc using these 5 dc (see images below). Sk 1 dc, ch 2, *sk 1 dc, 1 pc in ch1sp, sk 1 dc, ch 2**. Rep from * to ** across. Sl st to the first pc to join. Finish off Color C. [14 pc, 14 ch2sp]

The remainder of the project will be worked using Color A.

R4: With RS facing Join yarn with 1 standing dc in any ch2sp. Work 1 more dc in the same ch2sp. 1 dc in pc. *2 dc in the next ch2sp, 1 dc in pc**. Rep from * to ** around. Sl st to the first dc to join. Turn. [42]

The rest of the project with will be worked in joined rounds. Remember to turn at the end of every round. This will keep the seam line straight up the back of the hat.

Hat Shaping Section (we are decreasing the hat to fit to the top of the head).

R5: Ch 3 (counts as 1 dc), dc2tog. *1 dc in the next st, dc2tog**. Rep from * to ** around. Sl st to the top of the ch 3 to join. Turn. [28]

R6: Ch 3 (counts as 1 dc), dc2tog. *1 dc in the next st, dc2tog**. Rep from * to ** around to the last st. 1 dc in the last st. Sl st to the top of the ch 3 to join. Turn. [20]

R7: Ch 1, sk the st at the base of the ch 1, 1 hdc in the next st (together these count as 1 hdc2tog). *Hdc2tog**. Rep from * to ** around. Sl st to the top of the first hdc2tog to join. Turn. [10]

R8: 1 sc in each st around. Finish off leaving a 8-10 inch tail of yarn to weave in and close the top of the hat. [10]

Crochet Christmas Tree Hat Pattern

Sizes baby to adult large.

Supplies

Yarn: Yarnspirations. BERNAT Softee Chunky. 3.5 oz (100 g) and 108 yds (99 m). 100% Acrylic. Super Bulky Weight Yarn [6]. Machine washable and dryable.

Colors: 1 skein in Dark Green (28237)

Hook: 6.5 mm (K).

Finished Project Yardage: Child Size (6-10 years) hat: 100 g / 108 yds

Scissors, Yarn Needle, Stitch Marker, beads, balls, bells, ornaments, sewing thread or hot glue

Difficulty Level

Easy

Finished Size

Sizes available: 0 to 3 months, 3 to 6 months, 6 to 12 months, 12 mos to 3 years, 3 years to 5 years, 6 years to 10 years, adult small (teen), adult medium and adult large.

Gauge

Approximately 10 rows per 4 inches and 9 sts per 4 inches

You can substitute any yarn and hook for this stitch pattern – just remember when you substitute if your gauge is different, the finished size, and amount of yarn used for your project will also be different.

Abbreviations

US Terminology used

beg – beginning

BL – back loop

ch – chain

DMR – double magic ring

R – row or round

rem – remaining

rep – repeat

ps – puff stitch (see special stitches)

sc – single crochet

sk – skip

sl st – slip stitch

st/sts – stitch/stitches

* to **– Repeat the instructions between the asterisks the number of times indicated. This repeat will contain of multiple instructions.

[] – at the end of the row – the total number of stitches

() – important notes AND sets of stitches to be worked within one stitch, or space

Special Stitches

Puff Stitch (ps)

Insert hook into specified stitch, yarn over and pull up 1 loop (2 loops on your hook). Yarn over and insert your hook into the same stitch, yarn over and pull up 1 loop (4 loops on your hook). Yarn over and pull through all 4 loops. Notes:

You will want to use a stitch marker to mark you place as we are working in continuous rounds. We do not slip stitch to join at the end of the rounds.

When you are decorating your hats, please keep in mind who you are making the hat for. If you are making hats for babies and you add decorations please consider the hats as photo props only and never leave the baby unattended with the hat. If you are decorating them for toddlers, or small children, please do not leave your child unattended with the hat. Please be mindful of our little ones when you decorate and gift these finished hats. We would never want anything to jeopardize their safety. xo Rhondda

If you do not want to begin using a DMR, chain 2 and slip stitch to the second chain from the hook to create a ring and then work the stitches indicated in R1, into that ring.

The best part about this hat is if you gauge is slightly off you can simply keep repeating the pattern until your hat reaches the head circumference of the person you are making it for! If you work repeats of the rounds as listed and once you have a puff stitch round that measures the circumference of the head you want to fit – switch to the single crochet finishing rounds. Your hat might end up being taller, or shorter than mine did, but it should still look great and fit!

Baby (0-3 mos) Christmas Tree Hat

To fit 18 inch head circumference. Hat height approximately 9 inches.

The hat is crocheted in continuous rounds from the crown to the brow, in one piece.

Using your 6.5 mm (K) hook (or size required for gauge):

R1: DMR: 4 sc into the ring. [4 sc]

R2: 1 sc in each st around. [4 sc]

R3: 1 ps in each st around. [4 ps]

R4: 2 sc in each st around. [8 sc]

R5: *1 ps in the next st, 1 sc in the next st**. Rep from * to ** around. [4 ps, 4 sc]

R6: *2 sc in the next st (which is the ps), 1 sc in the next st**. Rep from * to ** around. [12 sc]

R7: *1 ps in the next st, 1 sc in the next st**. Rep from * to ** around.

[6 ps, 6 sc]

R8: *2 sc in the next st (which is the ps), 1 sc in each of the next 2 sts**. Rep from * to ** around. [16 sc]

R9: *1 ps in the next st, 1 sc in the next st**. Rep from * to ** around. [8 ps, 8 sc]

R10: *2 sc in the next st (which is the ps), 1 sc in each of the next 3 sts**. Rep from * to ** around. [20 sc]

R11: *1 ps in the next st, 1 sc in the next st**. Rep from * to ** around. [10 ps, 10 sc]

R12: *2 sc in the next st (which is the ps), 1 sc in each of the next 4 sts**. Rep from * to ** around. [24 sc]

R13: *1 ps in the next st, 1 sc in the next st**. Rep from * to ** around. [12 ps, 12 sc]

R14: *2 sc in the next st (which is the ps), 1 sc in each of the next 5 sts**. Rep from * to ** around. [28 sc]

R15: *1 ps in the next st, 1 sc in the next st**. Rep from * to ** around. [14 ps, 14 sc]

R16: *2 sc in the next st (which is the ps), 1 sc in each of the next 6 sts**. Rep from * to ** around. [32 sc]

R17: *1 ps in the next st, 1 sc in the next st**. Rep from * to ** around. [16 ps, 16 sc]

R18: *2 sc in the next st (which is the ps), 1 sc in each of the next 7 sts**. Rep from * to ** around. [36 sc]

R19: *1 ps in the next st, 1 sc in the next st**. Rep from * to ** around.

[18 ps, 18 sc]

R20: 1 sc in each st around. [36 sc]

R21-R22: 1 sc in the BL of each st around. Finish off with an invisible join. [36 sc]

Baby (3 mos – 6 mos) Christmas Tree Hat

To fit 18 inch head circumference. Hat height approximately 10 inches.

The hat is crocheted in continuous rounds from the crown to the brow, in one piece.

Using your 6.5 mm (K) hook (or size required for gauge):

R1: DMR: 4 sc into the ring. [4 sc]

R2: 1 sc in each st around. [4 sc]

R3: 1 ps in each st around. [4 ps]

R4: 2 sc in each st around. [8 sc]

R5: *1 ps in the next st, 1 sc in the next st**. Rep from * to ** around. [4 ps, 4 sc]

R6: *2 sc in the next st (which is the ps), 1 sc in the next st**. Rep from * to ** around. [12 sc]

R7: *1 ps in the next st, 1 sc in the next st**. Rep from * to ** around.

[6 ps, 6 sc]

R8: *2 sc in the next st (which is the ps), 1 sc in each of the next 2 sts**. Rep from * to ** around. [16 sc]

R9: *1 ps in the next st, 1 sc in the next st**. Rep from * to ** around. [8 ps, 8 sc]

R10: *2 sc in the next st (which is the ps), 1 sc in each of the next 3 sts**. Rep from * to ** around. [20 sc]

R11: *1 ps in the next st, 1 sc in the next st**. Rep from * to ** around. [10 ps, 10 sc]

R12: *2 sc in the next st (which is the ps), 1 sc in each of the next 4 sts**. Rep from * to ** around. [24 sc]

R13: *1 ps in the next st, 1 sc in the next st**. Rep from * to ** around. [12 ps, 12 sc]

R14: *2 sc in the next st (which is the ps), 1 sc in each of the next 5 sts**. Rep from * to ** around. [28 sc]

R15: *1 ps in the next st, 1 sc in the next st**. Rep from * to ** around. [14 ps, 14 sc]

R16: *2 sc in the next st (which is the ps), 1 sc in each of the next 6 sts**. Rep from * to ** around. [32 sc]

R17: *1 ps in the next st, 1 sc in the next st**. Rep from * to ** around. [16 ps, 16 sc]

R18: *2 sc in the next st (which is the ps), 1 sc in each of the next 7 sts**. Rep from * to ** around. [36 sc]

R19: *1 ps in the next st, 1 sc in the next st**. Rep from * to ** around. [18 ps, 18 sc]

R20: *2 sc in the next st (which is the ps), 1 sc in each of the next 17 sts**. Rep from * to ** around. [38 sc]

R21: *1 ps in the next st, 1 sc in the next st**. Rep from * to ** around. [19 ps, 19 sc]

R22: 1 sc in each st around. [38 sc]

R23-R25: 1 sc in the BL of each st around. Finish off with an invisible join. [38 sc]

Baby (6 mos – 1 year) Christmas Tree Hat

To fit 18 inch head circumference. Hat height approximately 10.5 inches.

The hat is crocheted in continuous rounds from the crown to the brow, in one piece.

Using your 6.5 mm (K) hook (or size required for gauge):

R1: DMR: 4 sc into the ring. [4 sc]

R2: 1 sc in each st around. [4 sc]

R3: 1 ps in each st around. [4 ps]

R4: 2 sc in each st around. [8 sc]

R5: *1 ps in the next st, 1 sc in the next st**. Rep from * to ** around.

[4 ps, 4 sc]

R6: *2 sc in the next st (which is the ps), 1 sc in the next st**. Rep from * to ** around. [12 sc]

R7: *1 ps in the next st, 1 sc in the next st**. Rep from * to ** around. [6 ps, 6 sc]

R8: *2 sc in the next st (which is the ps), 1 sc in each of the next 2 sts**. Rep from * to ** around. [16 sc]

R9: *1 ps in the next st, 1 sc in the next st**. Rep from * to ** around. [8 ps, 8 sc]

R10: *2 sc in the next st (which is the ps), 1 sc in each of the next 3 sts**. Rep from * to ** around. [20 sc]

R11: *1 ps in the next st, 1 sc in the next st**. Rep from * to ** around. [10 ps, 10 sc]

R12: *2 sc in the next st (which is the ps), 1 sc in each of the next 4 sts**. Rep from * to ** around. [24 sc]

R13: *1 ps in the next st, 1 sc in the next st**. Rep from * to ** around. [12 ps, 12 sc]

R14: *2 sc in the next st (which is the ps), 1 sc in each of the next 5 sts**. Rep from * to ** around. [28 sc]

R15: *1 ps in the next st, 1 sc in the next st**. Rep from * to ** around. [14 ps, 14 sc]

R16: *2 sc in the next st (which is the ps), 1 sc in each of the next 6 sts**. Rep from * to ** around. [32 sc]

R17: *1 ps in the next st, 1 sc in the next st**. Rep from * to ** around. [16 ps, 16 sc]

R18: *2 sc in the next st (which is the ps), 1 sc in each of the next 7 sts**. Rep from * to ** around. [36 sc]

R19: *1 ps in the next st, 1 sc in the next st**. Rep from * to ** around. [18 ps, 18 sc]

R20: *2 sc in the next st (which is the ps), 1 sc in each of the next 8 sts**. Rep from * to ** around. [40 sc]

R21: *1 ps in the next st, 1 sc in the next st**. Rep from * to ** around. [20 ps, 20 sc]

R22: 1 sc in each st around. [40 sc]

R23-R26: 1 sc in the BL of each st around. Finish off with an invisible join. [40 sc]

Toddler (12 mos – 3 years) Christmas Tree Hat

To fit 19 inch head circumference. Hat height approximately 11 inches.

The hat is crocheted in continuous rounds from the crown to the brow, in one piece.

Using your 6.5 mm (K) hook (or size required for gauge):

R1: DMR: 4 sc into the ring. [4 sc]

R2: 1 sc in each st around. [4 sc]

R3: 1 ps in each st around. [4 ps]

R4: 2 sc in each st around. [8 sc]

R5: *1 ps in the next st, 1 sc in the next st**. Rep from * to ** around. [4 ps, 4 sc]

R6: *2 sc in the next st (which is the ps), 1 sc in the next st**. Rep from * to ** around. [12 sc]

R7: *1 ps in the next st, 1 sc in the next st**. Rep from * to ** around. [6 ps, 6 sc]

R8: *2 sc in the next st (which is the ps), 1 sc in each of the next 2 sts**. Rep from * to ** around. [16 sc]

R9: *1 ps in the next st, 1 sc in the next st**. Rep from * to ** around. [8 ps, 8 sc]

R10: *2 sc in the next st (which is the ps), 1 sc in each of the next 3 sts**. Rep from * to ** around. [20 sc]

R11: *1 ps in the next st, 1 sc in the next st**. Rep from * to ** around. [10 ps, 10 sc]

R12: *2 sc in the next st (which is the ps), 1 sc in each of the next 4 sts**. Rep from * to ** around. [24 sc]

R13: *1 ps in the next st, 1 sc in the next st**. Rep from * to ** around. [12 ps, 12 sc]

R14: *2 sc in the next st (which is the ps), 1 sc in each of the next 5 sts**. Rep from * to ** around. [28 sc]

R15: *1 ps in the next st, 1 sc in the next st**. Rep from * to ** around. [14 ps, 14 sc]

R16: *2 sc in the next st (which is the ps), 1 sc in each of the next 6 sts**. Rep from * to ** around. [32 sc]

R17: *1 ps in the next st, 1 sc in the next st**. Rep from * to ** around. [16 ps, 16 sc]

R18: *2 sc in the next st (which is the ps), 1 sc in each of the next 7 sts**. Rep from * to ** around. [36 sc]

R19: *1 ps in the next st, 1 sc in the next st**. Rep from * to ** around. [18 ps, 18 sc]

R20: *2 sc in the next st (which is the ps), 1 sc in each of the next 8 sts**. Rep from * to ** around. [40 sc]

R21: *1 ps in the next st, 1 sc in the next st**. Rep from * to ** around. [20 ps, 20 sc]

R22: *2 sc in the next st (which is the ps), 1 sc in each of the next 9

sts**. Rep from * to ** around. [44 sc]

R23: *1 ps in the next st, 1 sc in the next st**. Rep from * to ** around. [22 ps, 22 sc]

R24: 1 sc in each st around. [44 sc]

R25-R28: 1 sc in the BL of each st around. Finish off with an invisible join. [44 sc]

Small Child Hat (3-5 years) Christmas Tree Hat

To fit 20 inch head circumference. Hat height approximately 12 inches.

The hat is crocheted in continuous rounds from the crown to the brow, in one piece.

Using your 6.5 mm (K) hook (or size required for gauge):

R1: DMR: 4 sc into the ring. [4 sc]

R2: 1 sc in each st around. [4 sc]

R3: 1 ps in each st around. [4 ps]

R4: 2 sc in each st around. [8 sc]

R5: *1 ps in the next st, 1 sc in the next st**. Rep from * to ** around. [4 ps, 4 sc]

R6: *2 sc in the next st (which is the ps), 1 sc in the next st**. Rep from * to ** around. [12 sc]

R7: *1 ps in the next st, 1 sc in the next st**. Rep from * to ** around. [6 ps, 6 sc]

R8: *2 sc in the next st (which is the ps), 1 sc in each of the next 2 sts**. Rep from * to ** around. [16 sc]

R9: *1 ps in the next st, 1 sc in the next st**. Rep from * to ** around. [8 ps, 8 sc]

R10: *2 sc in the next st (which is the ps), 1 sc in each of the next 3 sts**. Rep from * to ** around. [20 sc]

R11: *1 ps in the next st, 1 sc in the next st**. Rep from * to ** around. [10 ps, 10 sc]

R12: *2 sc in the next st (which is the ps), 1 sc in each of the next 4

sts**. Rep from * to ** around. [24 sc]

R13: *1 ps in the next st, 1 sc in the next st**. Rep from * to ** around. [12 ps, 12 sc]

R14: *2 sc in the next st (which is the ps), 1 sc in each of the next 5 sts**. Rep from * to ** around. [28 sc]

R15: *1 ps in the next st, 1 sc in the next st**. Rep from * to ** around. [14 ps, 14 sc]

R16: *2 sc in the next st (which is the ps), 1 sc in each of the next 6 sts**. Rep from * to ** around. [32 sc]

R17: *1 ps in the next st, 1 sc in the next st**. Rep from * to ** around. [16 ps, 16 sc]

R18: *2 sc in the next st (which is the ps), 1 sc in each of the next 7 sts**. Rep from * to ** around. [36 sc]

R19: *1 ps in the next st, 1 sc in the next st**. Rep from * to ** around. [18 ps, 18 sc]

R20: *2 sc in the next st (which is the ps), 1 sc in each of the next 8 sts**. Rep from * to ** around. [40 sc]

R21: *1 ps in the next st, 1 sc in the next st**. Rep from * to ** around. [20 ps, 20 sc]

R22: *2 sc in the next st (which is the ps), 1 sc in each of the next 9 sts**. Rep from * to ** around. [44 sc]

R23: *1 ps in the next st, 1 sc in the next st**. Rep from * to ** around. [22 ps, 22 sc]

R24: *2 sc in the next st (which is the ps), 1 sc in each of the next 21 sts**. Rep from * to ** around. [46 sc]

R25: *1 ps in the next st, 1 sc in the next st**. Rep from * to ** around. [23 ps, 23 sc]

R26: 1 sc in each st around. [46 sc]

R27-R30: 1 sc in the BL of each st around. Finish off with an invisible join. [46 sc]

Child Hat (6-10 years) Christmas Tree Hat

To fit 21 inch head circumference. Hat height approximately 12 inches.

The hat is crocheted in continuous rounds from the crown to the brow, in one piece.

Using your 6.5 mm (K) hook (or size required for gauge):

R1: DMR: 4 sc into the ring. [4 sc]

R2: 1 sc in each st around. [4 sc]

R3: 1 ps in each st around. [4 ps]

R4: 2 sc in each st around. [8 sc]

R5: *1 ps in the next st, 1 sc in the next st**. Rep from * to ** around. [4 ps, 4 sc]

R6: *2 sc in the next st (which is the ps), 1 sc in the next st**. Rep from * to ** around. [12 sc]

R7: *1 ps in the next st, 1 sc in the next st**. Rep from * to ** around. [6 ps, 6 sc]

R8: *2 sc in the next st (which is the ps), 1 sc in each of the next 2 sts**. Rep from * to ** around. [16 sc]

R9: *1 ps in the next st, 1 sc in the next st**. Rep from * to ** around. [8 ps, 8 sc]

R10: *2 sc in the next st (which is the ps), 1 sc in each of the next 3 sts**. Rep from * to ** around. [20 sc]

R11: *1 ps in the next st, 1 sc in the next st**. Rep from * to ** around. [10 ps, 10 sc]

R12: *2 sc in the next st (which is the ps), 1 sc in each of the next 4 sts**. Rep from * to ** around. [24 sc]

R13: *1 ps in the next st, 1 sc in the next st**. Rep from * to ** around.

[12 ps, 12 sc]

R14: *2 sc in the next st (which is the ps), 1 sc in each of the next 5 sts**. Rep from * to ** around. [28 sc]

R15: *1 ps in the next st, 1 sc in the next st**. Rep from * to ** around. [14 ps, 14 sc]

R16: *2 sc in the next st (which is the ps), 1 sc in each of the next 6 sts**. Rep from * to ** around. [32 sc]

R17: *1 ps in the next st, 1 sc in the next st**. Rep from * to ** around. [16 ps, 16 sc]

R18: *2 sc in the next st (which is the ps), 1 sc in each of the next 7 sts**. Rep from * to ** around. [36 sc]

R19: *1 ps in the next st, 1 sc in the next st**. Rep from * to ** around. [18 ps, 18 sc]

R20: *2 sc in the next st (which is the ps), 1 sc in each of the next 8 sts**. Rep from * to ** around. [40 sc]

R21: *1 ps in the next st, 1 sc in the next st**. Rep from * to ** around. [20 ps, 20 sc]

R22: *2 sc in the next st (which is the ps), 1 sc in each of the next 9 sts**. Rep from * to ** around. [44 sc]

R23: *1 ps in the next st, 1 sc in the next st**. Rep from * to ** around. [22 ps, 22 sc]

R24: *2 sc in the next st (which is the ps), 1 sc in each of the next 10 sts**. Rep from * to ** around. [48 sc]

R25: *1 ps in the next st, 1 sc in the next st**. Rep from * to ** around. [24 ps, 24 sc]

R26: 1 sc in each st around. [48 sc]

R27-R30: 1 sc in the BL of each st around. Finish off with an invisible join. [48 sc]

Adult Hat (small) Christmas Tree Hat

To fit 22 inch head circumference. Hat height approximately 13.75 inches.

The hat is crocheted in continuous rounds from the crown to the brow, in one piece.

Using your 6.5 mm (K) hook (or size required for gauge):

R1: DMR: 4 sc into the ring. [4 sc]

R2: 1 sc in each st around. [4 sc]

R3: 1 ps in each st around. [4 ps]

R4: 2 sc in each st around. [8 sc]

R5: *1 ps in the next st, 1 sc in the next st**. Rep from * to ** around. [4 ps, 4 sc]

R6: *2 sc in the next st (which is the ps), 1 sc in the next st**. Rep from * to ** around. [12 sc]

R7: *1 ps in the next st, 1 sc in the next st**. Rep from * to ** around. [6 ps, 6 sc]

R8: *2 sc in the next st (which is the ps), 1 sc in each of the next 2 sts**. Rep from * to ** around. [16 sc]

R9: *1 ps in the next st, 1 sc in the next st**. Rep from * to ** around. [8 ps, 8 sc]

R10: *2 sc in the next st (which is the ps), 1 sc in each of the next 3 sts**. Rep from * to ** around. [20 sc]

R11: *1 ps in the next st, 1 sc in the next st**. Rep from * to ** around. [10 ps, 10 sc]

R12: *2 sc in the next st (which is the ps), 1 sc in each of the next 4 sts**. Rep from * to ** around. [24 sc]

R13: *1 ps in the next st, 1 sc in the next st**. Rep from * to ** around. [12 ps, 12 sc]

R14: *2 sc in the next st (which is the ps), 1 sc in each of the next 5 sts**. Rep from * to ** around. [28 sc]

R15: *1 ps in the next st, 1 sc in the next st**. Rep from * to ** around. [14 ps, 14 sc]

R16: *2 sc in the next st (which is the ps), 1 sc in each of the next 6 sts**. Rep from * to ** around. [32 sc]

R17: *1 ps in the next st, 1 sc in the next st**. Rep from * to ** around. [16 ps, 16 sc]

R18: *2 sc in the next st (which is the ps), 1 sc in each of the next 7 sts**. Rep from * to ** around. [36 sc]

R19: *1 ps in the next st, 1 sc in the next st**. Rep from * to ** around. [18 ps, 18 sc]

R20: *2 sc in the next st (which is the ps), 1 sc in each of the next 8

sts**. Rep from * to ** around. [40 sc]

R21: *1 ps in the next st, 1 sc in the next st**. Rep from * to ** around. [20 ps, 20 sc]

R22: *2 sc in the next st (which is the ps), 1 sc in each of the next 9 sts**. Rep from * to ** around. [44 sc]

R23: *1 ps in the next st, 1 sc in the next st**. Rep from * to ** around. [22 ps, 22 sc]

R24: *2 sc in the next st (which is the ps), 1 sc in each of the next 10 sts**. Rep from * to ** around. [48 sc]

R25: *1 ps in the next st, 1 sc in the next st**. Rep from * to ** around. [24 ps, 24 sc]

R26: *2 sc in the next st (which is the ps), 1 sc in each of the next 23 sts**. Rep from * to ** around. [50 sc]

R27: *1 ps in the next st, 1 sc in the next st**. Rep from * to ** around. [25 ps, 25 sc]

R28: 1 sc in each st around. [50 sc]

R29-R33: 1 sc in the BL of each st around. Finish off with an invisible join. [50 sc]

Adult Hat (medium) Christmas Tree Hat

To fit 23 inch head circumference. Hat height approximately 14 inches.

The hat is crocheted in continuous rounds from the crown to the brow, in one piece.

Using your 6.5 mm (K) hook (or size required for gauge):

R1: DMR: 4 sc into the ring. [4 sc]

R2: 1 sc in each st around. [4 sc]

R3: 1 ps in each st around. [4 ps]

R4: 2 sc in each st around. [8 sc]

R5: *1 ps in the next st, 1 sc in the next st**. Rep from * to ** around. [4 ps, 4 sc]

R6: *2 sc in the next st (which is the ps), 1 sc in the next st**. Rep from * to ** around. [12 sc]

R7: *1 ps in the next st, 1 sc in the next st**. Rep from * to ** around. [6 ps, 6 sc]

R8: *2 sc in the next st (which is the ps), 1 sc in each of the next 2 sts**. Rep from * to ** around. [16 sc]

R9: *1 ps in the next st, 1 sc in the next st**. Rep from * to ** around. [8 ps, 8 sc]

R10: *2 sc in the next st (which is the ps), 1 sc in each of the next 3 sts**. Rep from * to ** around. [20 sc]

R11: *1 ps in the next st, 1 sc in the next st**. Rep from * to ** around. [10 ps, 10 sc]

R12: *2 sc in the next st (which is the ps), 1 sc in each of the next 4

sts**. Rep from * to ** around. [24 sc]

R13: *1 ps in the next st, 1 sc in the next st**. Rep from * to ** around. [12 ps, 12 sc]

R14: *2 sc in the next st (which is the ps), 1 sc in each of the next 5 sts**. Rep from * to ** around. [28 sc]

R15: *1 ps in the next st, 1 sc in the next st**. Rep from * to ** around. [14 ps, 14 sc]

R16: *2 sc in the next st (which is the ps), 1 sc in each of the next 6 sts**. Rep from * to ** around. [32 sc]

R17: *1 ps in the next st, 1 sc in the next st**. Rep from * to ** around. [16 ps, 16 sc]

R18: *2 sc in the next st (which is the ps), 1 sc in each of the next 7 sts**. Rep from * to ** around. [36 sc]

R19: *1 ps in the next st, 1 sc in the next st**. Rep from * to ** around. [18 ps, 18 sc]

R20: *2 sc in the next st (which is the ps), 1 sc in each of the next 8 sts**. Rep from * to ** around. [40 sc]

R21: *1 ps in the next st, 1 sc in the next st**. Rep from * to ** around. [20 ps, 20 sc]

R22: *2 sc in the next st (which is the ps), 1 sc in each of the next 9 sts**. Rep from * to ** around. [44 sc]

R23: *1 ps in the next st, 1 sc in the next st**. Rep from * to ** around. [22 ps, 22 sc]

R24: *2 sc in the next st (which is the ps), 1 sc in each of the next 10 sts**. Rep from * to ** around. [48 sc]

R25: *1 ps in the next st, 1 sc in the next st**. Rep from * to ** around. [24 ps, 24 sc]

R26: *2 sc in the next st (which is the ps), 1 sc in each of the next 11 sts**. Rep from * to ** around. [52 sc]

R27: *1 ps in the next st, 1 sc in the next st**. Rep from * to ** around. [26 ps, 26 sc]

R28: 1 sc in each st around. [52 sc]

R29-R34: 1 sc in the BL of each st around. Finish off with an invisible join. [52 sc]

Adult Hat (medium) Christmas Tree Hat

To fit 24 inch head circumference. Hat height approximately 15 inches.

The hat is crocheted in continuous rounds from the crown to the brow, in one piece.

Using your 6.5 mm (K) hook (or size required for gauge):

R1: DMR: 4 sc into the ring. [4 sc]

R2: 1 sc in each st around. [4 sc]

R3: 1 ps in each st around. [4 ps]

R4: 2 sc in each st around. [8 sc]

R5: *1 ps in the next st, 1 sc in the next st**. Rep from * to ** around. [4 ps, 4 sc]

R6: *2 sc in the next st (which is the ps), 1 sc in the next st**. Rep from * to ** around. [12 sc]

R7: *1 ps in the next st, 1 sc in the next st**. Rep from * to ** around. [6 ps, 6 sc]

R8: *2 sc in the next st (which is the ps), 1 sc in each of the next 2 sts**. Rep from * to ** around. [16 sc]

R9: *1 ps in the next st, 1 sc in the next st**. Rep from * to ** around. [8 ps, 8 sc]

R10: *2 sc in the next st (which is the ps), 1 sc in each of the next 3 sts**. Rep from * to ** around. [20 sc]

R11: *1 ps in the next st, 1 sc in the next st**. Rep from * to ** around. [10 ps, 10 sc]

R12: *2 sc in the next st (which is the ps), 1 sc in each of the next 4 sts**. Rep from * to ** around. [24 sc]

R13: *1 ps in the next st, 1 sc in the next st**. Rep from * to ** around. [12 ps, 12 sc]

R14: *2 sc in the next st (which is the ps), 1 sc in each of the next 5 sts**. Rep from * to ** around. [28 sc]

R15: *1 ps in the next st, 1 sc in the next st**. Rep from * to ** around. [14 ps, 14 sc]

R16: *2 sc in the next st (which is the ps), 1 sc in each of the next 6 sts**. Rep from * to ** around. [32 sc]

R17: *1 ps in the next st, 1 sc in the next st**. Rep from * to ** around.

[16 ps, 16 sc]

R18: *2 sc in the next st (which is the ps), 1 sc in each of the next 7 sts**. Rep from * to ** around. [36 sc]

R19: *1 ps in the next st, 1 sc in the next st**. Rep from * to ** around. [18 ps, 18 sc]

R20: *2 sc in the next st (which is the ps), 1 sc in each of the next 8 sts**. Rep from * to ** around. [40 sc]

R21: *1 ps in the next st, 1 sc in the next st**. Rep from * to ** around. [20 ps, 20 sc]

R22: *2 sc in the next st (which is the ps), 1 sc in each of the next 9 sts**. Rep from * to ** around. [44 sc]

R23: *1 ps in the next st, 1 sc in the next st**. Rep from * to ** around. [22 ps, 22 sc]

R24: *2 sc in the next st (which is the ps), 1 sc in each of the next 10 sts**. Rep from * to ** around. [48 sc]

R25: *1 ps in the next st, 1 sc in the next st**. Rep from * to ** around. [24 ps, 24 sc]

R26: *2 sc in the next st (which is the ps), 1 sc in each of the next 11 sts**. Rep from * to ** around. [52 sc]

R27: *1 ps in the next st, 1 sc in the next st**. Rep from * to ** around. [26 ps, 26 sc]

R28: *2 sc in the next st (which is the ps), 1 sc in each of the next 25 sts**. Rep from * to ** around. [54 sc]

R29: *1 ps in the next st, 1 sc in the next st**. Rep from * to ** around. [27 ps, 27 sc]

R30: 1 sc in each st around. [54 sc]

R31-R36: 1 sc in the BL of each st around. Finish off with an invisible join. [54 sc]

Finishing Instructions:

Weave in all remaining ends.

Decorate ! I used 1 strand of Beads and a Bag of Tiny Bells from Dollarama. I thread the beads through the spaces between the stitches from the bottom to the top of the hat. I hand sewed the bells onto the hat with sewing thread.

Optional Crochet Star for you Christmas Tree Hat

Make 2

The crochet star is worked in continuous rounds. Then you place 2 together with right-sides facing out and join them together with a slip stitch seam around the outer edges. Working slip stitches evenly around the outer edges, chaining 1 at the points and slip stitching into the main star center in round 3 when you reach the center between each point (working over the single crochet from the previous round and into the same stitch it was worked into in the round prior).

Supplies: Medium Weight Yarn [4] (Red Heart Super Saver) and a 4.5 mm (G) hook. You may also want to use a stitch marker.

R1: DMR: 5 sc [5 sc]

R2: 2 sc in each around. [10 sc]

R3: *1 sl st in the next st, ch 5. We are now working into the chain 5 you just made. 1 sc in the 2nd ch from the hook, 1 hdc in the next ch, 1 dc in the next ch and 1 tr in the last ch. Sk 1 sc from R3**. Rep from * to ** 5 times. Sl st to the first sl to join. Finish off (star 1). Do not finish off star 2, instead proceed to finishing instructions below. [5 points (1 sc, 1 hdc, 1 dc and 1 tr) and 5 sl st]

Finishing Instructions

Place the 2 stars on top of each other with the points lining up and the right sides (good sides) facing outward. Join your yarn through both layers of the star using a slip stitch and work slip stitches evenly around the star.

I worked 4 sl st up each point to the tip, chained 1 and worked down the other side of the point (4 sl st) to the round part of the star. Then I worked 1 sl st into R3 (the same st you put the sc into in R4 – I worked overtop of that sc and worked a sl st on top of it). I finished off with an invisible join (leaving about 10 inches of yarn) at the end and then attached it to the tree.

Hat Crochet Tutorials

Made in the USA
Las Vegas, NV
07 May 2021